ENGLISH SHORT STORIES
FOR INTERMEDIATE LEARNERS

100 ENGLISH SHORT STORIES
TO IMPROVE YOUR VOCABULARY
AND LEAN ENGLISH THE FUN WAY

English Language and Culture Academy

© Copyright 2018 by English Learner And Culture Academy - All rights reserved

License Notice

This document is geared towards providing exact and reliable information regarding the topic and issue covered. In no way is it legal to reproduce, duplicate, download, or transmit any part of this document in either electronic means or printed format without the consent of the author or publisher. Recording of this publication is strictly prohibited and any storage of this document is not allowed unless with written permission from the publisher.

All rights reserved

The information provided herein is stated to be truthful and consistent, in that any liability, in terms of inattention or otherwise, by any usage or abuse of any policies, processes, or directions contained within is the solitary and utter responsibility of the recipient reader. Under no circumstances will any legal responsibility or blame be held against the publisher or author for any reparation, damages, or monetary loss due to the information herein, either directly or indirectly. The information herein is offered for informational purposes solely and is universal as so. Any name and content in this book is fiction and not related to any real events or persons. The presentation of the information is without a contract or any type of guaranteed assurance.

Contents

Learning English Through Short Stories 6
Using This Book Effectively 7

1. The Key 9
2. What is Culture? 10
3. Food Poisoning 12
4. The Neighbor 13
5. Headache 15
6. A New Driver's License 17
7. New Year's Eve in Europe 18
8. Invoices and Contracts 19
9. World Traveler 20
10. Hobby Chef 22
11. The Break In 24
12. A Broken Phone 25
13. The Painters 27
14. Quitting 28
15. Swimming 31
16. Dialogue – The Weekly Farmer's Market 33
17. The Experiment 36
18. Dialogue - Bicycle Paths in a European City 38
19. New Neighbors 40
20. The Funeral 41
21. The ATM 43
22. Alcoholics 44
23. Cutting the Cable Cord 46
24. Foreigners in Britain 48
26. To the Airport 52
27. The Big Move 54
28. Driving and Parking in Germany 56
29. Grocery Shopping 58
30. A Clean House 59
31. Future Plans in Mexico 61
32. Dialogue - Dining European Style 62
33. Our Bicycle Tour 64
34. A Visit to the Doctor 66
35. The Spanish Restaurant 68
36. The Mysterious Lamp 70
37. Not Always Fish and Chips 72

38. An Unusual Marriage 74
39. New Shoes 76
40. Ticket Control 77
41. Unemployed 79
42. Divorced 81
43. Buses and Trains 82
44. A Famous Book 84
45. A Simple Salad 85
47. Vegan Food 88
48. Evacuation 90
49. Working Men 92
50. Under the Lamp Post 94
51. My Best Friend 96
52. Preparations 98
53. Social Media 100
54. Big Lenders, Big Spenders 102
55. Traffic and Kids 104
56. Down with the Pounds 105
57. Kindness 107
58. A Helping Hand 109
59. My Hobbies 111
60. Vacation is Important 113
61. Learning in a Group 115
62. Our New House 117
63. Studying Abroad 118
64. The Circus 119
65. The Car Accident 121
66. Our Hotel 122
67. In the Office 124
68. A Walk in the Park 125
69. A Special Credit 126
70. Winning the Lottery 127
71. The Application 128
72. Taxi Driver 129
73. In the Theater 130
74. The oakery 131
75. My Old Drivers License 133
76. Dialogue - Where is our Cat? 134
77. The First Time in England 135
78. A Happy Marriage 136
79. School and our Future Plans 137

80. I Marry my Office 138
81. Dialogue - Today we have Pigeon Meat 140
82. The Hermit 141
83. Retirement in Comfort 144
84. The Barbecue Evening 146
85. The Maid 149
86. The Merchant of Arts 151
87. A New World 153
88. AirBnB, The Mysterious Shadow and a Revolver 157
89. Adventures in the Spa 159
90. A Religious Family 162
91. Crowdfunding for a new Kitchen 165
92. How To Find a Millionaire on a Cruise Trip 168
93. A Visit From America 171
94. The Old Lush 174
95. The Treasure in the Woods 177
96. Au Pair in England 180
97. The Cheese Stinks from all Sides 182
98. Siblings 185
99. A New Recipe 186
100. Best Friends 187
101. A Postcard from Costa Rica 188
102. The Order 190
103. One Michelin Star is not Enough 192
104. The Allotment 195
105. Inexpensive Shopping in Japan 198
106. History - The First Humans 199

Learning English

Through Short Stories

Reading culturally interesting and entertaining short stories to enhance your English is an easy way to improve your English language skills. This book contains a selection of 100 short stories for intermediate level learners with a wide range of genres, all prepared specifically for English language students. This book aims to teach different English vocabulary and phrases associated with short stories and to improve your English language skills in a short time. All stories are written by an English linguist to ensure you can learn from authentic material while fine-tuning your English vocabulary and improving your comprehension.

The content is intended mainly for elementary to intermediate level learners, but it will also be useful for more advanced learners as a way of practicing their reading skills and comprehension of the English language. The stories have been arranged according to their degree of difficulty and each story is accompanied by a key vocabulary section and story related questions.

Using this Book Effectively

For beginners it's probably more beneficial to glance through the story first and then read aloud. Then review the key-vocabulary section and reread the story once more or until you get a grasp of the story. Then carefully read the story at your own pace until you understand each sentence. Vocabulary will be introduced to you at a reasonable pace, so you're not overwhelmed with difficult words all at once. Here, you won't have to look up every other word, but you can simply enjoy the story and absorb new words simply from the story's context. To learn English effectively you just read each story at a time and study the vocabulary after reading. the English presented in this book is British English, although some of the stories are based on American English.

The English contained in this book is written using easy-to-understand grammar and vocabulary that both, those at the beginner and intermediate levels can understand, appreciate, and learn from. Some stories are focused on dialogue. These stories contain loads of natural dialogue, so you can learn conversational English as you read. This is doubly beneficial as you will improve your speaking ability as well. Over time, you will build an intuitive understanding of how English functions. This differs from a more theoretical understanding put together via learning rules and conceptual examples. It's more important to reach to finish the story without stopping than to understand every word. The simple truth is that you won't get everything your first time around. This is completely normal. Towards the end of this book you find the stories slightly longer and more complex, but still comprehensible for beginners.

1. The Key

I'm late today and I have to leave for work very quickly; I am literally **jumping into my car**. As I turn onto the freeway, I'm suddenly not sure if I took my door key with me. I'm touching my bag. "My God! I forgot my key," **I say aloud.**

I make a u-turn and drive back as fast as I can. I park my car right in front of my door, although it's not normally where one is allowed to park or to stop a car. I live on the third floor and still run up the stairs hoping to get away with it. **I'm looking for the key** in my apartment but I can not find it right away. **After a few minutes**, I come to the realization: I had left the key in my jacket! I'm running downstairs back to the car. **I'm looking around.** Where's my car? In the distance I see a tow truck pulling my car off.

2. What is Culture?

I sit with several students in a café in Paris.

We have an international meeting. Americans, French, and Germans sit at a table and discuss.

The American asks, "**What does culture mean** in this country?"

I say, "That term can mean a lot. Literature, theatre, art, or even the way we speak, including **the way you conduct yourself**."

"Does it also include **behavior**? " asks the American.

"Behavior in general terms, probably is a part of it," says the German.

"So that means when I behave I have culture," ask the American smiling.

"More or less," I reply. "But **education and manners** would also describe culture"

"Can one say in France as well that I have culture, and you do not?" asks the American.

"No, **that would be arrogant,**" I assert.

3. Food Poisoning

My brother Marc feels terrible; he's been in bed **since yesterday**. He has nausea, a headache, coughing, and diarrhea. He also **feels exhausted**. My father drives my brother to the doctor. **He explains** the conditions to the doctor and the doctor examines Marc. The doctor finds out that Marc has **food poisoning**. It's a dangerous situation because Marc is already dehydrated! The doctor also prescribes that Marc stay in bed and take **strong medication** twice a day. My brother believes his food poisoning comes from a kebab he had eaten the day before when he stopped **downtown**.

4. The Neighbor

My mother and I are watching our **new neighbor**. Every morning at eight o'clock he leaves his house. We're **watching him** from the kitchen window. The man is young and wears a suit and tie. We think he's a man of class. He is always coming and going **at a particular time**.

My mother also has many friends and often **invites** strange men into the house as well. **The men are very friendly** and often give my mother **gifts.** After their visits, we sometimes have a lot of cash on hand. Just when the men have left, we usually **rush** to the mall **to go shopping**. One day we meet the new neighbor in the supermarket. My mother smiles at the man. They start talking. The neighbor comes to our house and **spends time** with my mother. A month later, my mother says, "we're going to move soon. We will live with Jeff, our neighbor, I **convinced** him to let us live with him."

5. Headache

Mrs. Meyer has **a severe headache**. The doctor examines her shoulder and prescribes the woman's pills that she has to take **every day**. In addition, the doctor gives the woman a list of **activities** to do. She **is supposed to do** yoga and meditation regularly, as the doctor states that the headaches come from stress.
The woman does the activities for **several days**, but the headaches do not go away. **After a week** she goes back to the doctor.

"Do you feel better? " asks the doctor.
She says no, and that she always gets a headache when she's **nervous.**

"**Do you sleep enough**?" he asks. She states that she doesn't know.

After further investigation, the doctor prescribes pills for nervousness, tablets for stress, and valium for sleeping. At home, Mrs. Meyer now has a big box full of pills and tablets.

6. A New Driver's License

Three days ago, I received my **driver's license**. With a driving license, **I can drive** almost any car in the United Kingdom, and in most other European countries as well. I received my license shortly after my 18th birthday. **It's important** that I can use my license **everywhere** because **I need to drive** to Spain soon.

Unlike in other countries, such as the US, the making of a driver's license in Europe can be **very expensive.** But **there are some differences** in Europe. For instance, in Germany, a driver's license is **valid** for as long as you live. Today I will be on the highway **alone for the first time,** driving my father's car, a Porsche. **I'm going to drive slowly** and leave the beer bottles at home.

7. **New Year's Eve in Europe**

New Year's Eve is always the night of December 31st in Germany, France, and Italy. Most people **celebrate** New Year's Eve with **friends and family. At midnight** there are always **fireworks**. Most families also prepare **a special meal**. A typical New Year's meal is carp, goose, or hotdogs; Germans also love potato salad. Often, New Year's Eve **is an occasion** for many people to drink lots of alcohol. Most young people also go to parties, and some even **go dancing**! On 1 January is a **holiday** all over the continent, with almost **all businesses closed.** On 2 January however, it's a normal **working day** in Europe.

8. Invoices and Contracts

I am a student from France and live in a small apartment **outside of** London. **Every month** I have to pay a lot of **bills. The rent** is an important bill and costs me **more than anything else**. Every month I pay the rent, the water bill, my phone, and the electricity bill. I usually have the bills automatically **deducted from my account**. If my account is empty, I will **wire transfer** the money. **Contracts** must be taken seriously, and are very important in England! If you **breach a contract** in this country you will certainly **get into trouble**. If your income is fluctuating it is probably best to avoid contracts.

9. World Traveler

I was born in Dayton, Ohio, but to tell the truth, **I never felt very comfortable** there. Fortunately, I **discovered** different countries when I was still a teenager. My parents **traveled a lot** and we were lucky to be able to live in different countries. For I can remember Asia, especially Japan, has always fascinated me. Europe is interesting, but most countries **are not easy to live in**, although the culture and especially the food was always the best. When I got a little older I started to travel by myself. I drove to Mexico and traveled all the way down to Panama. These were of course more **adventurous** than ordinary travels. I can honestly say that **travel is educating in many ways**. You also learn different cultures and I got quite good at developing

social skills. Most Americans travel only within their own country, and there is nothing wrong with that, but I feel that international experiences educate more and are good for the brain.

10. **Hobby Chef**

My name is Susanne and today I'm **going to show you** how to make schnitzel. I **prefer** beef steak, but many people **also like to eat** pork.

First I cut the beef into thin slices. Then I'll hit them with my flat hand **until they're right**. I sprinkle both sides with salt and pepper. I prepare three plates: on the first plate I have flour, the second plate a beaten egg and on the third plate I have breadcrumbs. The slices are first **laid into** the flour, then onto the egg, and finally turned onto the breadcrumbs. **The meat is fried from both side**s for 2 to 3 minutes in a frying pan.

English Short Stories for Intermediate Learners

11. The Break In

I have slept restlessly all night. I sleep alone and suddenly there's a bang. I jump out of bed. I put on a pair of pants and **examine** the house. I hear footsteps. They're coming out of the living room. **When I enter** the living room, it's empty. There's no one there. Now I notice that the balcony is open**! I turn on the lights** and look around.

The cupboards are open, and on the floor are all my things. There were burglars here! I feel bad, but quickly notice that there is nothing missing**. Everything is messy**, but the burglars didn't take anything. **They were looking for** cash and jewelry! I **believe** they were drug addicts because they only stole cash. I don't want to call the police; the next day, I'll get a gun.

12. A Broken Phone

I haven't been able **to charge my phone** for days. At first, I thought it was on **the charger**. This may not be the reason, because the charger also works with another phone. **Luckily,** I know a shop, where they can fix it. I have to leave the phone there for a day so it can be investigated. The next day, I go back to the business to pick up my phone.

I have a **strange feeling**. The **salesman** shows me my phone and opens it. Everything seems to be black! The man tells me the phone was damaged by a **short circuit**. **The repair** would cost two hundred dollars. He also says that the phone **has become wet**, and that's how it broke. Today he has an offer for a new phone. The new phone costs only three hundred dollars.

I have no choice but to buy a new phone. I'm never going to use my phone in the bathtub again.

13. **The Painters**

This morning the painters came. It was **overdue** as our house looked quite **dilapidated.**

The painters brought a ladder and started by painting the outside walls. Each wall must be painted with white paint. They **carry a bucket** of paint, a brush, and a roll. With a roll one can paint many walls in a short amount of time; only one day should be necessary for our small house. But they're **not done yet.**

Tomorrow the interior walls in the house must be painted. The painters **want to be paid immediately** in cash and with no questions asked.

14. Quitting

Next month Sammy is going to be thirty years old. The problem is**, he's been smoking** cigarettes for over ten years. He has tried all kinds of tricks and methods to stop smoking. Nothing has helped, and he knows **he needs treatment**. By chance, he has found out about a few small **uninhabited islands** that belong to the US beneath the Canadian border. There are no public ferries and they seem to be **the ideal place** to quit smoking!

After a week, Sammy is already on the island. He plans to stay a week until all the nicotine has left his body.
As he arrives he throws his last package into the bushes. After three days Sammy is almost bored to death. Interestingly, he finds an almost full bottle of whiskey in

the bushes. **He has nothing else to do** but drink the whiskey. **All of a sudden**, he begins hearing music! After investigating the source he finds an old man sitting in front of a **cave** listening to music and smoking a cigar.

"What are you doing here?" asks Sammy.

The old man is also **surprised**.

"I'm here to give up alcohol, and you?"

"I am trying to quit smoking. Is this your bottle of whiskey? "

"Yes. And **I imagine** this is your tobacco package, isn't it? "

Sammy nods. He feels very dizzy. "Listen, can I have my cigarettes back?"

"Of course, if you also give me the whisky bottle back."

In the end, **the men agree** and continue to do the things they did before.

15. **Swimming**

We are a group of boys and are **avid swimmers**. Most of us are twelve years old, and only our friend Peter is eleven.

Every Friday afternoon we go to the **public swimming pool.** First, we need to go to the **locker rooms**. There we change our clothing to proper swimwear, and after that, we'll take a shower. **Before and after** swimming one has to **take a shower**, which is obligatory in public swimming pools. Sometimes taking a shower takes quite some time, because we like to make jokes and are **fooling around**. Once in the swimming pool, we jump from the plank and swim around. We start with 1000 feet **breaststroke,** after that, we usually go on to twenty minutes of **freestyle**. Towards the end, we just play water ball. At the edge of the pool, **a lifeguard** is always there **observing** us.

Last week when we were finished swimming, we didn't shower afterward because an unknown child had left his excrements in the shower.

Short Stories based on Dialogue

16. Dialogue – The Weekly Farmer's Market

My family loves to buy fresh products from local farms; that's why we all go on Saturdays to the farmer's market. My husband is a hobby chef, and he only buys vegetables at the market.
Our favorite stand is at the end of the market where we can also buy fresh herbs.

"Good morning Lisa and Harry, so nice to see you again."
"Good morning Bill! What is the freshest thing you have today?"
"Harry, you know that all my products are fresh, everything has just arrived directly from the eco-farm."
"So, from all the tables and stalls here, you deliver them here first?"

"That's right. I am here at the entrance of the market that's why my tables come first."

"Okay Bill, then we will have two pounds of tomatoes, and about three pounds of potatoes. And also a bundle of carrots please."

"Anything else?"

" Do you also sell figs?"

"No, they don't grow around here."

"Ok, how much do I owe you?"

"That's six dollars total."

17. The Experiment

At school, Sandra asks her classmates: "Is it true that old people smell different?"

Her friend Gabi replies, "Well, they all smell rotten."

John laughs. "No, only the dead are rotten. Old people are not dead yet. They are still alive."

Gabi chuckles. "All right. Then we will call them mature. But as a matter of fact, I don't care how we call old people. I just don't want to be near them. "

John raises his hand. "Wait a minute. I once saw an experiment on YouTube. It shows that old people don't smell any different. Scientists let three groups of people sleep in shirts: old, middle-aged, and young. Each person had to sleep in the same shirt for five nights, and the shirts were not washed. Then they asked volunteers to smell the shirts. The volunteers didn't know which shirt came from what group, but all agreed said that the shirts of the old people smelled the best. "

"What kind of volunteers were these people who want to smell old people's shirts?" asks Sandra.

John: "They were, of course, old retirees."

18. Dialogue - Bicycle Paths In A European City

Last week I rode a bike to the university. There were two bicycle paths on the road. On the opposite side was a young girl. She looked very beautiful. She rode with me parallel in one direction.

Suddenly she stopped, and yelled at me: "You're driving on the wrong side!"

We both stopped. She came closer. "Don't you know the traffic rules?" she asked me.

I said, "I just wanted to save time."

She replied, "You don't save time if you hurt someone. An accident could damage your bike. You could end up in the hospital! You have to take your time. Accidents happen every day because people don't have time! Do you want to be hurt as well?"

I then ask her, "Are you married?"

19. New Neighbors

Since I moved into a new apartment, I've also got new neighbors. A family lives above us, and the children are still small. Sometimes I hear them play. At night, the parents are seldom at home and the children often scream strangely. A young man is living next to our apartment as well. He is a student and lives alone, except he keeps a cat in his apartment. When we meet in the stairwell he usually greets me. Next week we all have a so-called tenants meeting where all the tenants of the apartment meet and talk about common affairs. I'm looking forward to the meeting, as I will have my say about what's right and wrong within this building.

20. The Funeral

Last week, my grandma died. The whole family is very sad. The funeral will take place in the late afternoon, and perhaps some of the family will join together for a dinner at a restaurant. By tradition, most of the dead are buried but cremations are becoming more common, as some people think it's more practical. When people go to a funeral they meet in the church first. There everybody can see the coffin, nicely decorated with wreaths and flowers. The pastor makes a speech about the life of the deceased. Then everybody meets outside. The coffin is carried by the bearers to the tomb. The family and friends follow the carriers and at the end, the coffin is slowly dropped into a large hole. As a final goodbye, my parents and siblings throw earth on the coffin.

21. The ATM

Tomorrow is the weekend. I want to pay cash in the supermarket and go to the movies later. Before that, I have to go to the ATM to withdraw money.

First, I put my card in the ATM. A prompt will appear on the screen to enter my secret number. The secret number, also known as the PIN, is made up of four numbers. After that, I gain access to my account. I can also see on the screen how high my account balance is. I decide to withdraw fifty euros. After I withdraw the money, I have to take my card out. Finally, I get a receipt.

22. Alcoholics

Nowadays many people drink too much alcohol. Worldwide there are millions of alcoholics. That is why many people die of alcohol-related diseases such as cirrhosis. However, it seems everyone drinks alcohol in one way or another. It is socially acceptable, so the question is: how harmful can alcohol really be? Most doctors and experts agree that it is the daily amount that makes the most difference. Too much alcohol can damage many organs, especially the brain, the stomach, and the intestines. There are also many reasons why someone can become an alcoholic. Psychologists have found out that one of the main reasons someone grabs a bottle is loneliness and frustration. Defeating addiction can be very difficult, but it is also not impossible either. Most alcoholics can treat themselves by just cutting the amount or stopping by changing their behavior, but a doctor can also help with therapy. A special role can be played with the support of friends and family as well.

23. Cutting the Cable Cord

Over the years our cable TV subscription has become more of a burden than enjoyment. We are not rich and actually have to count every dollar carefully that we spend. One of the more unnecessary luxuries we treat ourselves to is cable TV. Our kids love it and my husband is watching sports and news channels all the time. However, our monthly bill is dangerously approaching the 200 dollar mark, something we no longer can ignore. Since no one in our family is very familiar with modern technology I had to do some research myself. Streaming TV via a so-called stick seems to do the trick. I convinced my husband to buy a smart TV and a little device called Roku. Ever since, we are all watching TV via streaming channels such as Sling, PlayStation Vue, and others; we are saving a lot of money as a result. Of course, nothing in life is free. We have to pay for the channels every month but they are still much cheaper than cable TV. The bottom line is this rather new technology is cheaper and we are also free from a constant bombardment of advertising.

24. Foreigners in Britain

In England, there are many landmarks for sightseeing trips and popular tourist destinations in general. Probably the most visited cities by foreign tourists are London, Brighton, Yorkshire, and probably Britain's most visited sightseeing spot is the mysterious Stonehenge. Most foreign visitors want to stay in London as there are hundreds of famous places to see. Westminster Abbey, Big Ben, the Buckingham Palace, Piccadilly Circus, and the British Museum are probably even some of the most visited places worldwide. London alone has over nineteen million visitors per year and since the British Pound has fallen sharply over the last few years, the UK will continue to be a very popular destination. The most common reason why foreigners like Britain is probably its culture, for instance, tea time, pub culture, and the Queen but also its history that seems to be everywhere and connected to everything in their culture.

25. The Tourist Guide

Carlos was born and raised in Veracruz, Mexico, but he has been living in New Jersey for over a decade. Since he had an accident and no one could help take care of him; he decided to go back to his country and live there with his family. Now he is a tour guide for American tourists in Cancun. When the cruise ships come there are virtually thousands of English speaking tourists who not only want to see the beaches and restaurants; but are keen to explore the countryside and what the surrounding culture has to offer. Carlos accepts group tours as well as individual tourists. He is quite popular and made himself a name as a knowledgeable guide, who has gained a small fan community on various online travel platforms. The tours usually start early in the morning and last until late afternoon. Many tourists wonder how Carlos speaks English without an accent. He tells them a little about himself, but that usually leads to more private questions. Carlos is not oblivious; for each question, he has prepared a perfect answer. This is something he had learned in the US.

26. **To The Airport**

Today begins my holiday and I will take a flight to visit my family. At eleven o'clock a taxi picks me up to take me to the airport. The taxi ride takes about one hour and will cost me around sixty dollars. After that, I still have enough time until my flight departs. I have already packed my suitcase. Packing is no child's game, with everything needing to be planned and considered. If I forget something, I will probably have to buy it at some expense at my destination.

It is already one minute before eleven and I am getting impatient. Finally, the taxi arrives. The driver helps me to carry my suitcase from the house to the car. I take the back seat and watch the meter charge me a dollar for every hundred yards or so. Sometimes they offer fixed rates but not this company; I think it's different in every city and state. Anyway, as we arrive I give the driver a tip since he didn't take unnecessary detours.

27. The Big Move

We have planned to move to another city. Everything has been planned for weeks, but this Friday we'll finally make the move. All our household items have been packed in boxes, most of the furniture has been carefully wrapped in blankets and foil. Additionally, we have made a list of which items are in which boxes; this will help us to save time when we unpack our stuff. It is difficult to make a move like this alone, which is why we have asked friends to help us. We also leased a truck for that day. Since we are doing everything ourselves, with a little help from friends and neighbors, we are saving a lot of money. Professional moving companies are expensive and we would rather save our money to buy additional furniture since the new house is larger than the old one.

28. Driving And Parking In Germany

I just moved to Germany. This is a country for cars; the highway is called Autobahn and these are excellent roads for high-speed car travel. Most Germans have a garage and some families even own several cars. But not all is perfect in this country; most Germans know that in the inner cities there is no free parking. If you are looking for a free parking space where you are also allowed to, you might drive around for hours until you find one. Parking garages can be very expensive, especially if you need one for a whole day or even long-term. People who live in the city often need to apply for a resident parking card. In this country, every resident needs to be registered with the authorities, which can be a good or a very bad thing. Those who cannot get a residence parking card but need to park their car in the centers have to leave their car on the fringes of the city and use public transportation.

29. Grocery Shopping

My name is Fatima. I am originally from the Middle East; but I am living in England where I have made myself quite comfortable, especially since I can live here with my family. Grocery shopping is one of my daily needs. Usually, I do this in the morning when fewer customers visit the supermarkets. To save money, I always prepare a list. For instance, today I need rice, vegetables, milk, sardines, and pasta. If I find cheap offers I buy more of it. Potatoes and pork are not on my menus very often, as it's something more for the British. In most supermarkets, you have to pack your bags yourself and you can pay with your credit card.

30. A Clean House

Once a year, I need to clean the whole house thoroughly, This happens usually in springtime when there is less moisture in the house. We are a rather large family with four children, all of them teenagers, so the mess and dirt are piling up quickly. Our house is a rather typical single-family house with an attached garage and a small attic. The living room is openly connected with the kitchen. We also have an extra freezer outside the house where we store meat. Some of it comes from the hunting that my father usually does on weekends. Anyway, when we start, we first clean the rooms of the kids. We clean the floor and wipe the windows; we need to mop the floor more than once until it shines and looks like new. I clean the furniture, and usually, I need about half a day to get the kitchen clean. My brother cleans the garage and helps to bring the trash out. We are a clean and functioning family with a clean house and healthy children. We are rightfully proud of ourselves.

31. Future Plans in Mexico

I am on vacation in Mexico and walking on the beach. I am staring at the sea. My thoughts wander into the future. What will my future be like? What I am supposed to do? I am dreaming of finishing my education with a doctoral degree in medicine. Then I really could become a doctor and work in a hospital. I could even have my own business. I also imagine becoming a plastic surgeon. I know they make a lot of money and most have an excellent reputation. Some of them even have become celebrities. My thoughts wander further. I could also finish my education with honors and then finish my life. But then again, I like where am I right now. Perhaps I should just stay here in Mexico and spend my life in a hammock.

32. Dialogue - Dining European Style

Unlike in the US, in many European countries, a customer can just enter a restaurant and choose an available seat where you feel comfortable. However, in more upscale restaurants most often there are no menus on the table, so you would have to ask the waiter to bring you one. The waiters usually wear a white shirt and black trousers. They also carry a little notebook to notate orders.

Often a conversation between a customer and a waiter follows this pattern:

Waiter: "Good evening, have you already found something that you would like to order?"

Customer: "I will take a schnitzel and a salad, number 5 on the menu."

Waiter: "That's okay. What would you like to drink?"

Customer: "Just mineral water."

Waiter: "With or without gas?"

Customer. "Still water, with little gas."

Waiter: "So you want a salad, a schnitzel and mineral water with little gas, correct?"

The customer nods.

After the meal, the customer asks: "The Bill please."

A tip is always voluntary and in most countries is not included in the bill.

33. Our Bicycle Tour

We are two young men on vacation in Holland. In this country, everyone has a bicycle and it's part of their culture; that's why we rented a bicycle for a whole week to explore not only big cities such as Amsterdam but also the countryside. From the early morning to late at night we are riding our bicycles and each day we try to cover longer distances. Normally we ride about fifty kilometers per day. There are no mountains to speak of so we can ride as fast as we can. Our bicycles are fully equipped, with head and tail lights, gear shifts, a bell, and even an air pump. Besides those, we also wear a helmet and a colored shirt. We'd like to think of ourselves as semi-professional bicycle riders. For me, it is more of a sport, but my friend already dreams of participating in the Tour de France.

34. A Visit to the Doctor

Elsa seriously thought she was pregnant. Her stomach already looked like she had swallowed a few basketballs when she decided it was time to call her doctor to hear the results from the last exams. But just like last time, the doctor confirmed that she wasn't pregnant at all. Still, over the next few weeks, Elsa gained more pounds. In addition, the shape of her stomach had become strange; it looked like a huge potato. The scale showed over 300 pounds and Elsa just couldn't find an explanation. Eventually, Elsa checked herself into a hospital for cosmetic surgery, basically to suck out the fat from her body. When Elsa left the hospital, she weighed only a hundred pounds. She asked the surgeon about her condition. The doctor pointed his finger at the lawn in front of the hospital. "Do you see that donkey on the lawn? We pulled that out of your body. Now you are healed."

35. The Spanish Restaurant

Frank has recently opened a restaurant in the Bay area, and his specialty is Spanish cuisine. Actually, the restaurant is part of his house that has also a large garden and is very spacious. One night, just when he wanted to close a young couple came in. His wife who works in the kitchen wondered why her husband is still letting guests in. "Frank, the kitchen is already closed; besides, we don't have enough in the refrigerator to cook two more meals." Frank shakes his head. "We do. I still have a rabbit in there. "

"But most people don't like rabbit," his wife complains. "I know a very old recipe from an old cookbook. Just let me try."

"How long does it take until you have cooked this recipe?"

"It will take about an hour. I still have to pull off the fur, since I shot the rabbit in the garden myself earlier."

36. The Mysterious Lamp

What Bruno Schmidt wanted to buy originally in this German flea market was a drum. He figured that to find a decent drum he had to go to a large flea market is in a major city and usually takes place on weekends. So, it was on Sunday that he saw a large red drum on a table that also offered a lot of broken stuff and old, seemingly useless items. For some reason, the vendor didn't want to sell him the drum.

"Can you not read," the old vendor asked him. He pointed his finger at a handmade sign that said: Take everything for 100 Euro.

It seemed the man didn't want to sell only the drum.

Then Bruno saw an old vintage lamp that looked really

interesting; a typical lamp with a shade that one would put into the bedroom. He could use a lamp like that. Bruno asked the man if he could buy the drum and the lamp together. The old man nodded. Bruno took a closer look at the lamp. There were old decoration lines on the lampshade which also had old pergament and bright color. Then he saw what looked like a long number in the corner of the shade. Was that a tattoo? "What is the lampshade made off," Bruno asked the man.
"I don't think it's animal skin," answered the man. "I bought it myself at the flea market in Buchenwald."

37. Not Always Fish and Chips

Molli runs a small restaurant in a small town in southern England. She sells fish and chips, but her most popular dish is hamburgers. She has been in the restaurant business for a long time, and since she is always eating her food in the restaurant she doesn't feel very healthy. She thinks all the grease and fried meals have taken their toll on her health. She tells this to some of her regular customers, and most agree she should offer healthier food. Other customers, however, have pointed out that she should keep her restaurant cleaner since there are a lot of cockroaches, sometimes they can be seen on the tables. Eventually, Molly buys several cookbooks about healthy food, especially exotic Asian food as it fascinates her. One day Molli has a brilliant idea. After a few days of trial and error, Molly sells Asian diet hamburgers. The customers like them, and some even think of them as fantastic. One regular customer asks Molly, what is the secret of this new and tasty hamburger? She tells him the meat is made of insects which is very common in Asia, and that she catches the insects all in her own restaurant.

38. An Unusual Marriage

Mr. Meyer is a public accountant but works in a large insurance company. He has an excellent reputation for being reliable and having a high work ethic. In a short period of time, he has risen to upper management. However, over the last few weeks, Mr. Meyer has often been sick. It also seems he is not very focused, with his colleagues saying that he is distracted by something. Mr. Meyer actually has a secret. For some time he has been engaged to his new girlfriend, but the real secret is that he met her on the street. The first time he met her, he paid for her time. One day he tells his colleagues that he plans to marry his fiance. One of his colleagues has always been suspicious and envious of him. After some research on the internet, he finds out that Mr. Meyer's fiance has a questionable past. He reports his findings to the directors. They give Mr. Meyer a choice. He can keep his job but he must not marry that woman, or he must leave the company. Mr. Meyer is desperate. Should he marry the woman or keep his job? Eventually, Mr. Meyer tells his bosses. "I will marry. But I am not going to marry the woman, I will instead marry my office if you give me a lifetime contract."

39. New Shoes

Today Gilbert is going to buy new shoes. In a shoe store, he asks the salesperson if they also have working shoes. The man replies that they have working shoes on sale for a special price. Gilbert sees a particularly nice pair of shoes on the shelf. He asks if they'd have these shoes in his size. The salesperson replies, "Sorry they come as they are, with no guarantees for shoes on sale." Gilbert checks the price and buys the shoe ad hoc. The next day Gilbert is wearing his new shoes. However, in the evening he comes back with one foot limping as his heal is wounded. His wife shakes her head. "Why did you have to buy shoes that are much too small for you?"
Gilbert replies. "Only one of them is too small, that's why they were such a bargain."

40. Ticket Control

I remember when I was a kid I spent some time in Germany; I even went to school there. In this country, trains are an essential part of daily transportation. We were a group of four children and it was winter with a lot of snow. Irma was one of the smaller children, at that time she was only eleven years old. We made a trip by train from Munich to a smaller city. It was a nice and modern train, and we had even our own compartment. We heard somebody knocking on the door. It was the ticket inspector, a man in uniform just to see if we had bought tickets. One by one he inspected the tickets, but Irma was nervously searching her bag; she couldn't find her ticket. The inspector asked for her identification, then told her to follow him. At that time the train had stopped at a little town. We waited for Irma to return but nothing happened. Suddenly the train moved and through the window, we could see Irma standing by herself frightened at the train station. But Irma looked different. Then we noticed that Irma was just standing there without her jacket! She had left it at her seat, and apparently, the inspector had kicked her off the train, letting her practically freeze to death at the station.

41. Unemployed

Laura finds herself unemployed again. For the last three years, she has been working as an accountant, but the company went bankrupt. The company she was with before has outsourced all the accounting to a company in India. Over the last decade or so, Laura has been employed on and off, sometimes with many jobless months in between. Nevertheless, Laura thinks of herself as a reliable, punctual, and trustworthy person and with a little luck, she thinks, she soon will be employed again. Every day she searches the classified employment websites and also the local newspapers for job openings. She sends out her resume to every company she can think of in the hope of work since unemployment diminishes her savings. One of her most important principles is to never give up. Her dream job is still being an accountant, but she knows times have changed. She is flexible, as finding work as a secretary would serve her as well.

42. Divorced

Last year I divorced my husband. My former husband is an alcoholic and cannot support his family. Fortunately, the children are already working, but still, they need financial support once in a while. I am meeting other divorced mothers at weekly meetups. Often we do excursions or share leisure activities. Some of my divorced friends will marry again, as it actually happens quite a lot. I noticed, if people stay alone too long, they become often alcoholics themselves. I have said goodbye not only to my husband but also to alcohol; I am on the best way to master my life anew.

43. Buses and Trains

Marco and Jane are siblings. Every weekend in the morning, they start a trip to visit their grandmother. Their grandmother lives in a distant city. Since the siblings don't have a car; they need to take public transportation, precisely the train and the bus. First, they have to take a communal train to the next major city. At the main train station, they have to take the metro train to get to the other side of the city. After that when they have finally arrived at the last station outside the city, they have to take a bus to get to their final destination; a village in the countryside. The whole journey takes about half a day and usually, they arrive just before lunch. After resting an hour or so, they leave and take the trip back to the city, taking the trains again just to arrive home at dinner time. They both save eagerly to buy a car, as a trip to their grandmother by car would just take about an hour.

44. A Famous Book

For about a month I have been reading a fascinating book written by a famous author. The book is a novel and is about an old man who goes out fishing in the ocean. He has to fight a large and mighty fish, and in the end, the old man wins this struggle. However, the book shows a deeper meaning. The author is Ernest Hemingway, who wrote the novel The Old Man and the Sea in 1951 in Cuba. This work is considered as one of the best in world literature. He was awarded the Nobel prize for world literature. I am fascinated by this book, and I'd love to read more from this author. I also think that good books are much better than movies.

45. A Simple Salad

Lisa works in a fine dining restaurant in London. She just started two weeks ago. Most often she works in the kitchen, but when the restaurant is busy she must also help out as a waitress. The chef is well known and a celebrity; and today he will work in the kitchen himself. Dinner service has started and the first orders are coming in. The chef shouts at Lisa: "I need a simple salad Lisa!" Lisa immediately starts to work on it. First she cuts lettuce and then mixes the salad with sliced cucumbers. She also chops a tomato in four pieces, cuts an onion, and a few olives into the salad. At the end, she mixes all the ingredients with olive oil, vinegar, salt and pepper. "The salad is ready," Lisa shouts out.

The chef looks bewildered at the plate. "This is what you call a simple salad?"

46. Easter

Easter in England and Europe, in general, is a holiday that involves the whole family. On Good Friday in the countryside, they often make bonfires where family and friends gather for some barbecue and sometimes music is played. The Easter Festival is a tradition in many countries.

For children, Easter morning is actually the most important day of the festival. In the morning hours, children love to paint hard-boiled eggs and hide them in the bushes. They make a game out of it to find the hidden eggs, but not all of the eggs are always found. Even weeks after Easter, there are times when the land stinks of rotten eggs that haven't been found.

47. Vegan Food

Maria knows that she needs to stay on a diet. She has read many diet cookbooks and does stretching exercises in the morning hours. She also has studied and experimented with many diet recipes, but a lot of recipes contain meat which Maria tries to avoid. However, cooking takes a lot of time, and whenever possible she tries to find a healthy restaurant, as she doesn't want to cook every day. A good friend of hers told her about a good vegetarian restaurant. Maria tries the restaurant and finds the dishes absolutely delicious. Almost all of the dishes are vegetarian, and some are even only vegan. After a short time, Maria has become a regular customer. Her favorite meal is a vegetable soup which is supposed to have no meat at all. One day she asks the cook why the soup is always so delicious, as she wants to know the secret. The cook answers that he is always using chicken stock.

48. Evacuation

We are retirees and live in a nursing home. Last fall we had a big storm. The storm was only the beginning. After it poured for days, the whole town became flooded. In the end, we had a power outage. The heating, electricity, and even the telephone was dead. At first, we took it lightly, but at night it got really cold with the temperature dropping below zero. It took three days until the buses arrived; they were supposed to evacuate us. To our surprise the buses did not pick us up, instead, they stopped next door where there's a luxury resort. They came first we were told, because they were able to charter the buses for a lot of money. We could not compete with the rates. When they left, the guests winked at us through the windows. We stayed in the nursing home, and fortunately, after a few more days the neighbors and private individuals evacuated us one by one.

49. Working Men

I used to work on a construction site and I would call myself a construction worker. In those days I had to carry a lot of heavy material, often bricks and cement. At times, I also had to clean asphalt manually with a broom. One day, a little girl approached me and asked me why I sweated so much. I told her, "It's because I have to work so hard." But she continued by asking me, why don't I do anything else. I replied, "Because I am only qualified for heavy labor." Suddenly my boss came and yelled at me. "What are you doing? I am paying you to work not to stand around."

I replied: "The girl was just asking me an innocent question."

"What did she ask you?"

"Why I was sweating so much."

"Enough," he said, "We are not a daycare center. Move it."

The next day I didn't return to work. I tried to find something else. Eventually, I found a good paying job cleaning sewers. The new job had one advantage; at least I didn't have to sweat that much.

50. Under the Lamp Post

Martin is studying in Paris and found a night shift job in a restaurant. Although he is studying and working hard; he doesn't feel quite at home yet. One reason is that he doesn't have any social contacts. He is more of a dreamer and still has to figure out how to spend his free time. Every evening when he comes home from work, he has to walk through a park. It is an empty large park, except for a few runners, there are not too many people. It's a beautiful park with typical French lanterns and benches. One evening Martin notices a woman standing by herself under a lamp post. She seems to be waiting for someone. Martin also thinks the woman is quite attractive. The next evening, the same woman waits again under the lamp post. At night when Martin goes to bed, he still thinks of the woman. A very attractive woman with light makeup and high heels. The situation occurs again and again over the next few weeks. However, Martin is too shy to speak to her, although sometimes he wishes he had more courage to do so. On a Friday evening, Martin approaches the woman. Today he is determined to talk to her. The woman receives him with a broad smile. She says, "Are you coming with me?"

51. My Best Friend

I have been friends with Rachel since high school. Now five years later, we are still in regular contact even though we live in different cities. When it comes to important things in life, we are always supporting each other. We both still have plans to continue at a specific university. This will be a perfect way to support each other again. My strong sides have always been mathematics and physics, while my friend prefers languages and the arts. Somehow, I always know what she doesn't and the other way around. At times we even support each other when we are anxious or upset. I had to calm her down a couple of times especially when she had trouble with her boyfriend. The bottom line is that we have an indestructible friendship which I hope will survive anything.

52. Preparations

My name is Nico and next Friday I will celebrate my birthday in my new apartment. I am going to be 30 years old. In the morning hours, my family will come to visit me. My parents will come with my siblings and grandparents. In the evening I will meet all my friends, as they all have received an invitation. Actually, I have invited them to stay for dinner as well. My mother is going to help me since I am a rather poor cook. She will prepare some chicken or meat, and most importantly she promised to bring a big cake. The cake must be decorated with thirty candles! I think it will be a custom-made cake from a bakery that also does artistic cakes. I heard that he doesn't accept all customers, which makes me smile.

Anyway, this will be a really important birthday party for me.

53. Social Media

My name is Nicole. The most important aspect of life to me is looking and feeling healthy. Being beautiful is also a part of my business. A few years ago, I started an online business where I sell cosmetics and perfume. To expand my business, I use different social media platforms to spread the message such as Twitter and Facebook. Additionally, I use powerful visual social media; my favorites are Instagram and Pinterest. I try to spread the word on how women can stay young and beautiful. Interestingly I receive a lot of new virtual friends, and it seems like everyone wants to connect with me. In the end, many customers also become friends, or sometimes even business partners. I have never regretted going back to my old job as a sales clerk. My life, my friends, and my money are coming from my online business.

54. Big Lenders, Big Spenders

After work I sometimes go to a pub. Usually I order a large beer and if there's a chance I'll watch a football match. Most men who go into the pub are regular customers, and some of them I know personally. For me, it's always fascinating to learn about their different backgrounds. There is one customer that I believe has come there every day for years. He likes to talk about himself; that he is a successful businessman, and that he is a wealthy man. One day he's asking me for a favor. He asks if I can lend him 50 pounds. Normally I am not someone who lends money easily. Anyway, he told me that I'd get it back tomorrow so I gave him the money. The next evening he showed up in the pub and he gave me back my money without much ado. A week passed by, and that old customer asked me again for money. Again I gave him some, as I expected to get paid back the next day, just as before. Strangely the next evening the man did not show up. I asked the bartender and other customers if anyone had seen the man. I was dumbfounded when I found out that yesterday the man borrowed money from many people, sometimes hundreds of pounds. We gave it to him because he paid us back before. However, we never saw that man again.

55. Traffic and Kids

Our son is already six years old. It's time that he learns some of the traffic rules since he loves riding his bicycle through the neighborhood. We tell him, if he crosses a street he must look to his right side first. Then he must check his left side, and only when no cars are coming is he allowed to cross the street. Especially when he sees a stop sign or a traffic light he must be very careful. If he sees a red light for pedestrians, he must stop and wait until it turns green. Some areas even have a few bicycle lanes, something that is kind of new to us, but even with those lanes, kids must be careful to use them and never speed!

56. Down with the Pounds

Recently Maria has gained some weight. Every morning she weighs herself on a scale. Yesterday the scale hit at over two hundred pounds, almost to the limit. She feels a little ashamed of herself especially since everyone else in her family is rather slim. For Christmas she expects all of her family to come for a visit. Her parents and siblings are worried about her weight problem. Maria has told them not to worry because she is working on a new diet plan which she has received from a good friend. Simply put her new diet consists of new cooking recipes.

Her family encourages her to keep the diet consistently. When Christmas finally arrives, she gets into an argument with her parents. They accuse her of not keeping her diet since they cannot tell if Maria has lost or gained weight. About a month later, Maria sends her family photos of herself. The pictures show the scale at her feet. Amazingly, she weighs only one hundred and twenty pounds. All of her family congratulates her on what a wonderful job she had done. However, Maria has a secret. For the photoshoot, she has manipulated the scale and just turned it back a little.

57. Kindness

Steven is a movie buff. Today is Friday and for this evening he plans to go to a theater to watch a newly released movie.

Steven arrives at the theater early, but there is already a long line in front of the box office. Interestingly, there are also many elderly people waiting in line. That's probably because on weekends they also show a few classic movies. Although the movie Steve wants to see starts in a few minutes, he offers an elderly couple to go before him. He understands well that it must be hard for them to stay in line, especially because of the rainy weather.

Steve is still staying in line as he sees a piece of paper on the floor. He takes a closer look and discovers that the paper is a twenty-dollar bill. He picks up the money and wonders if somebody in front of him might have dropped it. The elderly couple watches him. Suddenly they approach him. "It might well be that we just dropped the money by accident. But since you are such a kind person, it's all yours."

58. A Helping Hand

Steven is fifteen years old. From Monday to Friday, he goes to school, and around one o'clock he takes the bus home. Usually, the bus is crowded with other students. Sometimes the elderly take the bus too, as many of them are just too old to drive a car. Steven is a kind and compassionate young man. If he sees an elderly person riding on the bus, he offers his seat, because for older people it can be very hard to stand on a moving bus. At the bus station, there is a traffic light for pedestrians. It has a new system where one has to push a button to get a green light. Many elderly have trouble with this and Steven never hesitates to help old people to cross the street. Steven already has an idea of what he wants to do in the future; he thinks it would be very rewarding work if he could become a professional caretaker.

59. My Hobbies

My name is Miriam and I have many hobbies. The reason is simple; I just have many different interests. As a kid I had a large doll collection, but now my likes have changed. Nowadays I am very much interested in art. I like to paint and I am especially fond of reading books. I read all kinds of nonfiction books, even history. I also like to play the piano. Music is one of my favorite pastimes. Being involved with many hobbies is a tradition in our family. My sister likes to read books about philosophy and everyone in my family participates in cultural activities. Besides reading and music, I also like to play tennis and on special occasions, such as on vacation, I like to play golf. My parents are much more into animal breeding. My father is an expert with dogs and exotic animals. If time allows, I love to travel. However, I consider myself more of an explorer than a typical tourist. Having many hobbies and doing a lot of sports keeps my mind and body active, and helps me to look forward in life as well.

60. Vacation is Important

My name is Astrid. I have planned my vacation for over six months. I am from Sweden and the winters are terribly dark and cold there. I have not made a career choice to speak of, but I have saved enough money for an extended vacation in Southern Europe. Vacation is something I take very seriously and I try to plan as early as possible. That's because during school holidays and especially in the wintertime the airlines raise airfares disproportionately.

Next month, I will begin my winter vacation; I will fly to the island of Teneriffa, which is a part of Spain, but is located far out in the Atlantic Ocean. I am really excited about my upcoming vacation, as vacation time for me is the most important time of the year.

61. Learning in a Group

My name is Sofia. For about three years I have been living in Texas. I came here from Honduras with my whole family. My brother-in-law has resided in the US for many years and is a government employee; that's why the rest of the family was able to immigrate to the US. There is violence in my home country, but the reason we wanted to settle in North America was that the wages are much higher and life is more convenient in general. In a language school, I am trying to improve my English. Sometimes I don't understand everything that's being said. Then I ask the teacher, "Can you speak more slowly please?" Actually, my English has improved a lot since I am learning in a group. It is just more fun and engaging learning in small groups. I am glad that I have the opportunity to learn proper English in a country where sometimes it is not even necessary.

62. Our New House

My dad had bought a big new house for all of us. The house has three floors and on each floor, it has eight rooms. It also has a large attic which my dad plans to rent out. My dad explains to me that it is not easy to find reliable and affluent tenants. This weekend he is expecting some applicants. Last weekend we already had some applicants but they were not qualified; the first family was unemployed and the second family wanted to bring in a sick grandmother. My dad prefers to wait until he finds the right people. He says it's best to have single persons without family and non-smokers.

63. Studying Abroad

My name is Cliff. I am from the US and I would like to study in Germany. I have excellent grades, but for admission to a German university, I'd need to speak sufficient German. With a language exam, such as the DSH or TESTDAF I can prove my expertise. However, if I apply for an international major, a German language exam is not necessary. Then I am allowed to improve my German language skills in a regular language course. Fortunately, I already speak some German.

64. The Circus

Today I went with my mother to the circus. The show started at six, but we arrived early because we knew there would be a long line at the ticket box. My mother asked why the tickets are so expensive. The salesperson explained that they have big animals such as tigers, etc. and they need to eat enormous amounts of meat every day. Finally, the show starts. First, we see a clown who makes jokes by gesturing with his hands. Then a huge cage is set up and the animals arrive. We see an elephant that raises a leg, a monkey that is dressed in a girly school costume, and then we see the big cats led into the cage. A tiger has to jump through a burning ring, and a lion has to jump from stool to stool. I ask my mother if the animals are also doing such things in nature. My mother responds that she doesn't know.

65. The Car Accident

Last month I drove home from work just as I do every day. I was driving slowly and stopped at a traffic light. Suddenly, I heard a loud bang. The car behind me had hit my bumper. I immediately got out of the car and saw that the taillight was broken. The driver admitted his guilt immediately and offered me money for the damage. He wanted to give me five hundred dollars cash. I rejected his offer and told him I was going to call the police. Suddenly all around me went black. I have no memory of what happened at that moment. I awoke in a hospital. The doctor told me somebody had shot me from behind.

66. Our Hotel

We have just arrived at our hotel. This year we will spend our vacation in Spain. We have booked an all-inclusive hotel and the check-in was very efficient. The friendly receptionist gave us the room key after we paid a security deposit. We are from England. At first, it seemed the hotel had a very high standard. The rooms were spacious and everything looked great. The next day things started to turn out different. We discovered fat cockroaches in the bathroom and the closets were dirty. We bought travel insurance, but unfortunately, they don't pay for dirty rooms. My husband had an idea. He took pictures of the closets and cockroaches. In a nearby pharmacy, we asked for medication against diarrhea. I immediately contacted the insurance company and informed them that we have all become sick because of the unclean room. I attached a photo of the medication and the receipt. A few weeks later the insurance had refunded our stay.

67. In the Office

My name is Tonya and I am a secretary. I am usually very busy, especially on Mondays. In the morning, I have a 30 minutes drive to the office. First I make coffee and then I begin taking phone calls. When my boss comes in, I have to do him a personal favor. Afterward, I am usually feeling bad. Later in the day, I bring the mail to the post office; and in the afternoon I am cleaning the office. When I get home around 7, I need to go buy groceries. During the week, I often go to bed early. Sometimes I dream of my boss. Actually, I like my boss, partly because he always buys me gifts.

68. A Walk in the Park

Tom and Liz are good friends. Every Sunday they take a walk in the park for a couple of hours. Usually, Tom picks Liz up at home.

Today is Sunday and it's also Tom's birthday; he just turned thirteen. Tom has an idea. He knows her parents are not home today and goes to visit her early. He knocks on Liz's door and she opens it. "Why are you early? I am not ready yet."

"You don't need to be ready for a walk."

"What do you mean, Tom?"

"I came to visit you at home. Just let me in, and the rest you can imagine."

69. A Special Credit

For years, Jane had been planning to acquire a new car. The problem was that she was unemployed and still lived at her parents' home, strictly speaking in the basement. She run an online business, but that was not nearly enough to save money for a used car.

Her parents weren't interested in helping her, because they considered her old enough to earn her own money. With or without help she needed that car! On Monday morning Jane stood in the middle of an intersection and waved glossy pamphlets at cars. Jane was begging for money.

However, at midday she met a neighbor who changed her life. The man felt sorry for her and gave her his old car.

70. Winning the Lottery

My dad and I heard that my uncle had won the lottery. The game is called six of forty-nine, which means my uncle had to guess six correct numbers. We all think my uncle has become a millionaire. However, my dad explains that my uncle still has $2000.00 of debt owed towards our family. We decided to visit my uncle. As he opens the door he smells like alcohol. He tells us he never won the lottery, but that he had bragged about it in a bar. He just wanted to show off! My dad still demands his money. At the end of a long conversation, my uncle gives my dad his car. By doing that, he has paid his debts.

71. The Application

Last month I lost my job because I had an argument with my boss. I just left the office and went home. In my desperation to find a new job, I went to an employment agency. They said I am qualified for many different positions. I agree with that statement because I think of myself as an honest, dedicated, and diligent worker.

Every day I send out new applications and many of them I send via traditional mail to catch the attention of potential employers. However, most companies are not even answering. Yesterday I received a letter. The letterhead looked quite familiar, then I looked at the sender. I couldn't believe it! Apparently, my former company had fired my old boss, and now they are offering me the same position I had before.

72. Taxi Driver

Steve Jones is a taxi driver. He is a very hard working man. He drives his taxi for at least twelve hours a day. Sunday is the only day when he doesn't work. Although his job is very demanding, he meets a lot of different people. Many customers like to chat with Steve. Besides, he is driving a large limousine, and that makes the job more bearable. Many of the customers leave him a large tip. He cannot complain about the money. However, in the future, he would like to do something else. Steve has been thinking a lot about what he should do in the future. The other day he felt inspired. Now, he has a pretty good idea of what he is going to do after he quits this job. He has gotten the inspiration after he watched the movie "Taxi Driver," starring actor Robert De Niro.

73. In the Theater

This weekend the theater is showing a truly interesting film. It's supposed to be a romantic movie. That's the reason I have invited a neighbor to accompany me, as she also likes romantic movies. We buy popcorn and have a seat in the last row. Actually, the movie has many romantic scenes with some of them being quite strong. The woman leans her head on my shoulder. I take her hand and let it rest on my lap. Suddenly the woman becomes angry, gets up, and leaves the theater. I smile and watch the rest of the movie. For me, it was a lovely evening.

74. At the Bakery

My work shift starts in fifteen minutes. Before I get to my workplace, I like to stop at a local bakery to buy a sandwich. As I open the door, there is already a long line of customers. There are at least eight people in front of me. They buy everything from cakes to fresh french bread. I have to be in the office in less than ten minutes. Then comes my turn. Suddenly, an old man cuts the line directly in front of me. I say, "Excuse me, would you please stay in line!"
The old man as well the sales clerk is ignoring me. The old man is having a chat, and he wants to buy something that takes a long time to pack. I feel the heat rising in my head. I grab a cake and throw it into the face of the sales clerk. He drops to the ground while everybody screams

and runs to the exit. Then I am alone. I take my sandwich and leave.

75. My old Drivers License

Yesterday I turned seventy. I have been driving without any accidents for as long as I can remember. I always drove by car, even short distances, and I cannot imagine living without a vehicle. The reason I have never had an accident is because I always drive very carefully. This morning, there was a roadblock and the police examined every vehicle. They asked me to step out of the car. The officer told me I cannot drive a car anymore because it appeared that I never had a driver's license to begin with.

76. Dialogue - Where is our Cat?

One morning we found a dead bird lying in front of our door. It looked like someone placed it there.

I told my mother: "I think our cat Mika did this."

My mother answered: "That's nature, we must not interfere."

I disagreed. "That's dangerous."

"Why?"

"The dead bird carries bacteria. Mika will bring that bacteria into our house."

"You are right", said my mother, concerned.

My mother had to make a decision. She took the cat into the house.

After that I never saw Mika again.

77. The First Time in England

This morning I finally arrived by plane, for my first time in England. I am going to stay here for about a year. I came here to find work. It seems as though this country is very well organized. There is a lot of public transportation available and the streets are clean. The cars drive on the left side of the road. The supermarkets are well stocked also. I think the British are very polite people. I have noticed courtesies such as waiting patiently in line and apologizing on every occasion. It seems to be very common. In my country, the people are also nice, but more affectionate.

78. A Happy Marriage

My name is Berta. For over eight years, I have been married to Helmut. He is a successful businessman and I am a homemaker. We don't have children, but we do a lot of things together. My husband is very romantic and takes good care of me. However, we also have our differences. My husband likes sports and regularly goes to the gym. I, on the other hand, like to get up late and enjoy watching TV. Unfortunately, I am overweight, but I have promised my husband to start a diet. Recently, he came home early and caught me in the basement where I was indulging in candies.

79. School and our Future Plans

Sabine goes to school. Her teacher would like to know what the students want to do in the future as a profession.

"What profession would you all like to have in the future?" asks the teacher.

Micheal is the first to raise his hand. "I'd like to become a doctor, so I can cut open bodies and see what's in there."

Lukas nods and raises his hand. "I want to become a police officer, so I can shoot the bad guys."

Nicole is laughing as she goes next. "I would like to become a pilot, then I can feel as free as a bird."

Finally, it's Sabine's turn. "I want to become a teacher. I would like to help students be able to make good decisions about what they want to become in the future."

80. I Marry my Office

Mr. Meyer is an accountant and works for a large company. He has regular working hours. Mr. Meyer starts his day at eight o'clock and at five o'clock he leaves his office. Lately, Mr. Meyer seems ill. His colleagues say that he does not seem focused. What nobody knows is that Mr. Meyer has a secret. A short while ago Mr. Meyer met his new girlfriend and the real secret is that he met her on the street. As a matter of fact Mr. Meyer has paid money for her time.

One day, Mr. Meyer tells his colleague that he's going to get married soon. But this colleague who has observed Mr. Meyer and thinks he knows something, tells the boss that Mr. Meyer plans to marry a woman of questionable reputation. The boss tells Mr. Meyer that he is no longer allowed to work for the company when he marries this woman.

Mr. Meyer thinks carefully about his options. Should he marry the woman or keep the job? Finally, he tells his boss, "I am going to get married, but not to this woman, instead I will marry my office. "

81. Dialogue - Today we have Pigeon Meat

Fernando has a Spanish restaurant in Tokyo. The is the restaurant is part of a large house where he also lives. Behind the house is a large, wild garden. One night, when Fernando just wants to close his restaurant, guests came in late. His Japanese wife works in the kitchen. She wonders why her husband wants to serve customers so late. "Why do you still want to serve guests," she asks. "It's late and I'll never get out of the kitchen again."
"The guests have already ordered wine," says Fernando. "Plus, we still have pigeon meat in the fridge. So I told the guests tonight that I only have pigeon."

82. The Hermit

Some people say Michael Gomez is a hermit, but that's only partly true.

The truth is, he is living isolated in Andalucia near the city of Granada. A hermit is often poor in material things and this also applies to Michael. He has no electricity. But he can get some for cooking as he has a stove and in front of his house, he has connected a generator.

There is enough water; in the back area of his dwelling water virtually flows off the roof and down the wall until it disappears in the floor. Otherwise he is well equipped. He has a big be, and a homemade camping toilet.

Once a week he drives with his bicycle to Granada where he goes shopping in the supermarket. Michael has a dream, he wants a modern toilet and, even more important, a real, closed panorama window. The problem is, his dwelling has several smaller entrances and at the front a huge, over five meters wide entrance. The entrance is opened most of the time because no door fits and plastic foil doesn't help if it's cold and raining outside.

But the view out of this enormous entrance is fantastic. Michael lives surrounded by mountains and wood and from here he can look at a wide valley and the opposite mountains. The view inspires Michael. One day he wants to become an architect, if this doesn't work, maybe writer or artist.

One more problem is that no door and no window fits into the unusual form of this huge entrance. Friends say that it's impossible to install a panorama window there because Michael is living in a cave where ten thousand years ago bears and Neandertal people used to live.

83. Retirement in Comfort

Mr. Logan is an international salesman. He is traveling all over the world to sell computer software. The company he works for belongs to the most important companies in its field. Actually, the biggest companies of the world such as Exxon Mobile, BMW, Thyssen, Siemens, and even Airbus belong to his client base. Although Mr. Logan is making excellent money, he would like to have his own business. Mr. Logan is making a life-changing decision. He decides to leave his company and start his own business. He wants to sell products from various companies and use his old contacts to get started. Unfortunately, things don't work out as expected. His old customers don't accept his new products, instead, they prefer to continue to do business with his old company.

Fortunately Mr. Logan had saved enough money to retire in comfort.

84. The Barbecue Evening

Marco and Paula have children who still live in their house, but the couple has been separated for a short time. Fortunately, Marco still has a little flat in the city and has left the house to Paula and the children. Paula's parents are already eighty years old and have a silver wedding anniversary at the weekend.

It's a beautiful, warm summer afternoon and Paula's father Alberto has an idea. Why shouldn't they arrange a barbecue evening in the garden Marco, Friends, the kids, and relatives – all of them would come. Besides, Alberto has always liked Marco. After all, they are both hunters in a hunting club. Break-up or not, it would be a great barbecue evening.

Alberto calls his daughter and expects a promise for the weekend.

It costs Paula a lot of conviction that Marco should be the grill master in his own garden.

Marco agrees. Saturday in the afternoon the moment has arrived. The grill is turned on while the children are playing and the adults are drinking beer.

Music is blasting out of an old stereo. Alberto helps Marco at the grill although it is difficult for him and he had forgotten his glasses. Suddenly it comes into Marcos' mind that he has a present for Alberto.

It's a big hunting knife with a horn handle!

Marco explains that this is a very special knife from the traditional Spanish brand Muele. A knife for collectors!

The beautiful evening has come to an end. As Marco is about to leave, Paula gives him a kiss and says that she wants to talk to him the next day. On Sunday Marco and Paula meet again. She feels very grateful for the splendid barbecue evening.

They have a conversation and Marco tells her, that during their relationship not everything has been bad. Paula proposes to Marco; for the children, they could live together again.

Indeed, after one week the family moves together again. Marco is very happy, especially because the cheap knife which he bought on his single vacation in Thailand didn't fail to make an impression.

85. The Maid

Maria comes from Poland and works twice a week as a maid in a big house. The house belongs to Ms. Sanchez who is living alone. Once in a while, her son comes for a visit. Her son is unemployed and receives some money from his mother.

The son lives at a friends' place. He often comes in the morning hours to his mother's house and is watching TV. If the weather is fine he sits on the terrace and drinks beer. Maria has to carry the empty beer bottles into the basement. In the basement are huge numbers of cases with full beer bottles stored.

Ms. Sanchez works very hard. She works in a factory and comes home very late. But she often calls her son and also sometimes Maria.

One day the son asks Maria for a favor. He says: "I'll be on a trip to another country for a few weeks. But don't tell it my mother. Make it appear as everything is normal.
"No problem", says Maria.
The next few days everything seems to be normal. Ms. Sanchez calls Maria and asks if her son still was at home and if all is okay.
"Yes, Ms. Sanchez, everything is alright." Maria is sitting on the terrace and drinking beer. She'll carry the empty bottles in the basement.

86. The Merchant of Arts

In former times Werner Schultz was an actor in a theater. In Berlin he was well known, and also had managed to get an important role for a television series in which he acted as a credible criminal.

Mr. Schultz apparently was never poor and had always been interested in art and antiques.

Now he was over fifty years old and received fewer offers from movies and theaters. But Mr. Schultz had also become quite famous as an art painter.

It can be said that Mr. Schultz was a real artist and also a connoisseur of art, because he had wide knowledge, especially of antique paintings. He was well acquainted with the Impressionists of the 19th century. After many years as an artist, actor, and painting expert, Mr. Schultz was a welcomed customer in many shops and galleries.

Mr. Schultz bought many valuable oil paintings and antiques in antique shops and art galleries.

But his reputation for being a good supplier was even greater. The quality of his paintings and the merchandise he offered to sell was outstanding.

One day newspapers reported that the famous art dealer and actor Werner Schultz had died. No one knew that he had died since Mr. Schultz had no relatives, therefore journalists were looking for friends and relatives.

Recently, journalists found out what they were looking for Mr. Schultz was a distant relative of Hermann Göring.

87. A New World

To this day, Ben Iglesias has not been able to explain it. What had really happened? His life was no worse than before. But the strange thing was, that the feeling of not belonging here was not going away. However, that was not important anymore.

It all began with the return flight from Mars to Earth, a journey that had been planned for a long time. For his crew of four it was their first trip, for Ben it was already his fifth.

As they entered the earth's orbit, flickering light appeared for a couple of seconds, alarm signals were ringing everywhere. And then he lost consciousness.

When he woke up his crew was dead and the spacecraft was on emergency electricity, but the strangest thing was that the spacecraft had already landed and all the instruments were dead.

It was impossible to see how much time had passed since the accident. The weather, the coordinates, the data of the ship could not be correct. More important was the fact that there was no contact with the base. Everything seemed dead.

For a couple of seconds, Ben looked out of the window. Where was the Caribbean Sea? He was supposed to fly over Cuba, but under the ship, everything was yellow and brown.

Ben exited the spaceship and saw a white desert until the end of the horizon. It was very hot and the atmosphere had only 60% oxygen.

Suddenly, he could not believe what he saw. Slowly but surely, a group of humans approached. They surrounded him and said nothing. Ben was not afraid, because they did not look aggressive, but completely different.

The people were small, they were women and a couple of men and they looked like .... burned? Were they Australian Aborigines? There was some resemblance, but they were very thin, almost like skeletons and small as children. They gave Ben water and signaled him to follow the group. After a long walk, they came to a valley of stones, covered with small holes that were entrances to giant dark caves. From somewhere down there came the sound of water.

That was Ben's first impression. How long had he lived here now? Ben estimated that he had already lived with these creatures for about three years. At first, the language was the most difficult part. Now they were like his family. His wife was four heads smaller than him, but it worked. She always smiled at him. Life was no longer important. Ben felt good, his wife had the eyes of a black cat and every day she laughed more, she had become pregnant.

88. AirBnB the Mysterious Shadow and a Revolver

Anna loves AirBnB, It's already the third time that she spends her holidays in an Airbnb apartment.

Anna has rented a large apartment for an entire month, the owner spends most of his time in his room. watching TV. One night Anna returns home, the television in the owner's room is blasting on high volume.

Anna knocks on the door but nobody answers. She opens the door, enters the room, and screams. Anna stares at the old man who is sitting on the couch. His eyes and mouth are wide open. His head is covered in blood. In his hand he holds a revolver, the man has been shot.

For the police, it is clear suicide and the body is quickly carried away. Anna couldn't go home, because she couldn't change her flight and so she decides to stay the rest of her holidays in the apartment. But nothing is as before. Anna cannot sleep at night. To find sleep Anna smokes a joint before going to bed. One night she wakes up, she sees a large shadow approaching her bed. Anna can't move nor scream. The shadow leans over her and lies down on her body.

Darkness. Suddenly, sunlight shines through the window. Anna wakes up and feels bad. She's depressed. Was it a nightmare? At the bedside table, she sees something dark. Anna takes it and it felts quite heavy. Now she's recognizing it, it is the old man's revolver.

89. Adventures in the Spa

Mr. Schmidt is a businessman. He owns a small restaurant at a railway station and sells fish and chips there.

He has many regular customers because most of the customers like his dishes.

In the after-work hours, he frequently goes to a spa to calm down and relax.

Some time ago Mr. Schmidt went again to the sauna. Actually, it is spa facility with a steam sauna and Turkish bath which can be found in most of the major cities. They are furnished with several saunas and a swimming pool. That day the temperature of the herbal sauna seemed to be especially high. Mr. Schmidt had already been seating and sweating on the sauna bench, when the door opened.

A man came in. Mr. Schmidt recognized him immediately. It was a customer.

However, he didn't like this customer. Once the customer had denounced him because he thought that the restaurant was dirty.

The other man also recognized Mr. Schmidt.

The man smiled: "Good evening, Mr. Schmidt how are you?"

"Everything is well, thank you," answered Mr. Schmidt.

"Sweating cleans the body." said the man.

Mr. Schmidt had enough for the day and left the sauna. He went for a shower. This time Mr. Schmidt took a long shower, because he had gotten annoyed by the man.

After the shower Mr. Schmidt went into the changing room, a big room with many lockers. The towels were hanging on a hook. Mr. Smith toweled himself, the towel was wet but he felt better now. Mr. Smith left slowly the sauna area.

The client, he met in the sauna, was standing outside at the door.

The man looked at Mr. Schmidt and smiled: "Excuse me, Mr. Schmidt, but you have used and taken my towel!"

Mr. Schmidt shook his head. "No, I don't think so."

"Please have a look at your bag." said the man.

Mr. Schmidt opened his bag and pulled the towel out. The other man still smiled. "Look here, in the corner of the towel I have written some letters with a black pen.

"A.H." asked Mr. Schmidt.

"That's me." said the man.

90. A Religious Family

In a small city in southern Spain lives a German family. Ingo is twelve years old, Estefani is one year younger. They are both intelligent children and also very modern. They love to play on the internet and are passionate video gamers. Their parents are both educationists, their father works in the hospital and the mother is independent and has a small psychiatric office. It is Christmas time and Christmas songs are blasting out of the shops and supermarkets.

Although the siblings are conservatively educated they don't feel like Christmas.

In the last years, when distant relatives visited them, there were a lot of arguments. Last weekend, on a catholic holiday a colleague of their father came for a visit. Anyhow a dispute started. Seemingly it was about church or religion.

The siblings found out that their parents had the intention to go to the Christmas service in the church. An unfamiliar situation because usually the parents never go to church, except on Christmas though.

However, their mother's opinion is that in a little town there is a lot of tattling and it would be better to adapt and to show up for Christmas at church. Furthermore, it confesses to be a good person. Estefani and Ingo think differently though.

At Christmas, the siblings want to stay at home. Ingo preferably wants to participate in a live game on the internet and Estefani has got some duties to do on Facebook. A dispute arises; the parents blame the children to be badly educated and not having any manners. After the discussion, the parents are counseling. What shall they do? The mother has an idea. Why shouldn't they meet other psychiatrists at the office and talk about that with some colleagues?

The parents have some telephone conservations and in the evening the small group of pedagogues and psychiatrists meets for a change of views at the office. Ingo and Estefani are surprised, as their parents return from the meeting and explain that they don't have to go to church at Christmas.

Estefani wants to know why the parents have changed their opinion. The mother answers that the colleagues had analyzed them and it turned out that both of them were just a tiny little bit sick for their parents would be just a little religious and religion fundamentally is a kind of brain disease.

91. Crowdfunding for a new Kitchen

Melinda is a young girl from California. For years, she had been planning to acquire a new kitchen. The problem was that she was still living at her parents' home, strictly speaking in the attic.

There was a little kitchenette, like in a hotel, equipped with a microwave oven and a coffee machine. Melinda had always loved to rummage in cookbooks and had already downloaded hundreds of recipes and to be honest, she was a good chief. Her parents weren't interested in modern kitchens. However, why? They always ate American plain meals that usually consisted of fries, beans, sausages, and coarse ingredients.

Because Melinda was already thirty years old, her family did expect that she finally found a partner, married, and founded a family. But there was a problem for Melinda. She didn't have work and unemployment makes life difficult, as everywhere. With work or without – she needed that kitchen.

She had saved six hundred dollars. Around the corner was a huge home center that always had discounts for kitchens on Mondays. But that wasn't all. Hardware stores, just like supermarkets, can be places where you can often meet neighbors and friends. On Monday morning Melinda stood in front of the main entrance and waited.

Indeed, after twenty minutes the first neighbor came. Melinda didn't hesitate.

She told the old woman that she urgently needed to buy a pressure cooker because the old one was broken and she needed thirty dollars for a new pot. After a while, the woman gave her the money. It perfectly worked; Melinda met half a dozen neighbors and acquaintances, and on midday, she had enough money for

92. How to Find a Millionaire on a Cruise Trip

My name is Birgit and it all begins tomorrow. Packing the luggage is no cakewalk and although I've been preparing for weeks, I have currently problems keeping a clear head. I need to know what I can take with me and what I have to leave at home. I have just read that I must not take any bottles or groceries.

The cruise starts in Italy. No real cruises are starting in Germany except river cruises like they have on the Danube or Rhine, but they are exclusively for retirees. My cruise ship vacation will begin tomorrow evening.

It's an enormous vessel with several swimming pools and many restaurants. The idea to book a cruise ship vacation came to my mind when I recently met an old friend. She had already spread the news on Facebook that she had finally found her dream man.

Life can be beautiful. After ten years of online dating, my overweight female friend has finally found a boyfriend. He must be a rich guy since now I know how much such a cruise trip costs. My trip had cost over five thousand Euros, but my friend's voyage must have been even more expensive. My thoughts are wandering between packing and posh guys, cocktails, and toiletries. It's better to have plenty of them.

Tampons and shampoos fortunately don't weigh a lot. I hear the doorbell ringing. Who might that be, I have no time!

Hello, Andrea! What a surprise!"

"Hello Birgit, I just wanted to say the last time hello before you start your cruise trip tomorrow. May I introduce you to my fiancé? This is Bobo from Manila."

"I'm pleased to meet you"

"Hi!"

"Does he speak English?"

"His English is very good. After all, he had worked on the cruise ship where I met

93. A Visit from America

Berta and Willi are pensioners, they are from Hamburg but spend most of their time in Bavaria, a state in southern Germany. Many years ago they had bought a country house in a village.

The couple comes from modest families. Willi had worked as a bus driver and his wife Berta used to work in a supermarket.

One afternoon the doorbell rings.

Willi opens the door and in front of him stands a man with two children. Strangers.

"Yes?" "

The man responds in a language he doesn't understand.

Willi calls his wife. Berta greets the people who keep

talking enthusiastically, but Berta and Willi don't understand a word.

"I think they speak English", says Berta.

The children are shaking their heads but seem somehow encouraged to keep talking.

Suddenly, the man puts his hand in his pocket and takes a black and white picture out. He shows it to Berta and Willi. Willi puts his glasses on and nods kindly.

The family gets excited and the children embrace Willi. They speak in their own language and seem to be happy.

The man points at the cuckoo clock and then he points with his finger to his chest.

Berta smiled. "He seems to possess the same."

The children go into the kitchen and open the refrigerator.

Berta and Willi are following them.

"Are you hungry", asks Berta.

"Today we have sauerkraut with sausages. I'll warm it up for you."

The children are kissing Berta and the strange man shakes Willi's hand. At dinner they ate and laugh and suddenly, Willi understands a few words from the strangers.

"America, grandfather!" Willi and Berta agree, but the foreigners all speak at once

Suddenly, the family gets up and kisses Berta and Willi goodbye. The strange man gives a photograph to Willi. Willi nods kindly. The family finally leaves. Willi looks at the image again."It must have been the former owner when he was young".

"Yes, but who were these people?"

94. The Old Lush

The people of Chieti thought that Marta comes from an insignificant town in the center of the Italian Abruzos region.

The people also said, that she was speaking with an accent and lots of elderly people even said, that she originally came from Romania.

Sometimes Marta went to a restaurant to eat and there everyone was talking about her; sometimes she could even hear people saying that she lives with her grown-up daughter, a young woman who allegedly goes to London next summer to study

It was also well known, that Marta owned a dachshund named Max, with whom she'd take a walk at least once a day. Most of the people thought she didn't work. Marta had an open secret, she loved drinking wine. One to two bottles of red wine per day and she preferred to drink the wine alone.

In the early afternoon, she began to drink and continued drinking until evening started.

Better than going to the pub and losing her reputation there, she thought. She partly had lost her reputation because in the local supermarket Aldi she could regularly be seen with a shopping cart full of wine bottles.

What the people were interested in, was what kind of work she had, and why she lives alone. Sometimes she also seemed to be making a journey.

One day before Christmas a dark vehicle parked in front of her house. Men and women in uniforms; was it the police? We didn't know.

Interestingly a few days later another vehicle parked in front of the door. This time it was a white Van. Marta wore on this dark winter's day her sunglasses and got hastily inside the vehicle and the car disappeared. A neighbor claimed that the

95. The Treasure in the Woods

Jan Schulz is a romantic person. Although he has been already 18 years old at that time, he was more interested in history books than in young ladies, other than his friends and classmates.

When he didn't sleep or he wasn't busy with his homework he used to doze on the sofa and was dreaming of having lots of money one day. One afternoon he fell asleep on the couch. He had a lively dream.

He dreamed to have found a treasure on an island. As he found the chest, he opened it and a little cloud of smoke came out. The smoke formed itself into a mouth and an old voice said: Get up, go to the forest, you'll find a map there. The map will be buried beneath an old pine tree.

Dig a hole where you'll see some smoke fuming. It's a treasure map. You can become rich if you find the map. The smoke came closer to his face, all of a sudden Jan couldn't breathe anymore, and he thought to be choking. Jan remembered that this day was Sunday and it must already have been afternoon.

It was already autumn, fog racked over the landscape. Behind the house a path began, which lead directly to the forest. He followed the track and he didn't even go one hundred meters, as he already saw the pine tree and besides he could see fine, white smoke rising to the sky. Jan dug into the soil and found a little tube and inside he found a rolled-up scroll.

It looked like a Buddhist map or a scroll. He rolled it up and went home.

The next day he went directly after school to a shop, where gold and other objects of value could be sold. He didn't get any money for the map. John went home, lied on the couch, and fell asleep. He dreamed that he would never need any money. As he woke up he glanced smiling at the treasure map. The money and the treasure weren't important to him anymore.

96. Au Pair in England

The French parents of Nicole meant well with their daughter. They wanted to send her daughter as an au pair to England to learn English. An agency had organized accommodations for Nicole with an English family. The agency had charged the parents a lot of money for a one-month stay, but it didn't matter since their daughter's education was most important. Nicole was excited because she had never been out of the county before, and she would love to learn a new language.
It was August when Nicole traveled to England. However, when Nicole arrived she was in for a nasty surprise. She was not allowed to make phone calls and in the house, there was no internet. Therefore, Nicole had to go to the post office to send her parents a message. In the

end, Nicole had returned to France before the parents could receive it. The parents were very happy to see their daughter again and of course, they wanted to know if Nicole could speak fluent English by now.

The daughter explained: "No, I have not learned English since the host family spoke more Hindu than English. They were immigrants from India."

"This means that the whole trip was in vain," stated the mother. "No, not at all,"

97. The Cheese Stinks from all Sides

Harold Johnson had fallen in love. For a few weeks, he has had a new girlfriend; a woman who he met in the library and who told him she worked in the morning at the farmer's market at the cheese stand.

Mr. Johnson had a lot of free time in the afternoons, so he spend most of his leisure time in the library.

Mr. Johnson and the woman had a common hobby. They both loved to read classic literature and cookbooks in the library. Once, Mr. Johnson invited the woman to his home for a glass of wine. That's how they became a couple. However, the relationship was not without its problems. Mr. Johnson didn't like the smell of the woman. He told her quite frankly that she smells like cheese. Mr. Johnson believed, every time after the woman had visited him, his whole house smelled like cheese.

She explained to him that the smell must have come from something else. Eventually, she tells him when they first met she had to tell him that she had some kind of job because she felt embarrassed that in fact, she was unemployed. Mr. Johnson was glad to hear that. So he explained to the woman that, in reality, he was not a pensioner as he had told her before.

Mr. Johnson still doesn't understand why she always smells like cheese.

"So what's your real job then", asked Mr. Johnson the woman.

"I am unemployed but I do foot massages," she said.

"That explains the smell", Mr. Johnson replied.

"And what do you do for a living", asked the woman.

"I work on a farm in the pig stall, but fortunately only in the morning."

98. Siblings

Alberto and Maria are siblings. Every weekend they go to visit their grandmother. She lives in another city on the outskirts of a major city, so they need to go early. To be able to visit her, the siblings have to catch first the train and then the bus. When they reach the main station they have to transfer the train to reach their final destination. Usually, it takes about an hour until the other train arrives. When they finally arrive in the small town, they have to take the bus. The entire trip usually lasts three hours and by evening they have to return home.

99. A New Recipe

Molli is the owner of a small restaurant in a small town. She sells mainly fries and hamburgers. Most of the customers also like her food but some complain that the place is not clean and cockroaches running all over the place. Molli has plans to change her restaurant. It is going to be clean and offers healthy dishes. Molli has bought a cookbook containing many Asian and diet recipes. Molli is inspired to change her menu. The following days Molli adds vegetable hamburgers to the menu. A customer asks what the hamburger is made of and Molli responds that it is made of bread and ground meat made of insects. She had prepared the ground meat herself, killing and using all the insects she can find in the restaurant.

100. Best Friends

Since I was going to school, Sofia has been my best friend. We were about twelve years old when we first met. Even though she lives in another city, we have always maintained good contact. Later we even went to high school together. As far as I can remember we have always supported each other. I always have been good with languages while my friend is good at math. Sofia has always helped me with my homework and I helped her with learning French. As teenagers, we often consulted each other about boys' and women's issues. I hope we are going to be best friends for the rest of our life.

101. A Postcard from Costa Rica

Ms. Graham has ordered workers to her house to fix her heating. Ms. Graham lives alone and is glad when the men finally arrive around noon. The team consists of only the boss and one apprentice. The men start working and finally find a broken valve. The boss wishes to show the broken part to Ms. Graham and explain to her a few things, but Ms. Graham surprises the man with a few shots of Tequila for a break.

She raises the glass, "Gentlemen, before you continue, have a drink first." After five minutes, Ms. Graham comes back and insists on another round. The men obey and drink. Eventually, the boss orders the apprentice to head back to the office to get a replacement part. When after over an hour later the apprentice finally comes back to

Ms. Graham's house nobody answers the door. The next day the boss is not to be found in the office. The boss has disappeared! After about a week, mail arrives at the office; among it is a postcard from the boss. The postcard comes from Costa Rica and the boss lets his workers know that he is on a honeymoon with Ms. Graham.

102. The Order

A couple from Ohio is on vacation in Miami. They are sitting at a beachside restaurant and are ready to order. Finally, the waiter comes. He brings two menu cards and then disappears. The couple looks at the menu and is not impressed. There the man discovers dried-up Ketchup remains on the menu and shakes it with disgust. The waiter takes his time to serve other guests first and finally returns to the table with two glasses and water. He holds the glasses with his fingers on the edges, puts them on the table, and disappears again. The woman says to her husband. "I can see his fingerprints on the glasses. That's disgusting. Can you tell the waiter to bring us two other glasses?"

"But then the waiter wants to know why and we would have a serious discussion."

"Then ask him if he can bring us two closed water bottles."

"For that, we would need to pay extra. But I have an idea; I think we still have water bottles in the car. I'm going to get them."

"Good Idea. Please also bring the soap and a cloth so we can clean up the table before the waiter returns."

103. One Michelin Star is not Enough

The two brothers, Marc and Michael, are skilled restaurateurs, educated in a restaurant school in Switzerland. Both have already worked in established French Restaurants, and also have built a good reputation.

Ten years ago, they opened their first restaurant in London. From the beginning, the restaurant went well, and it took only a few years until the restaurant was awarded its first Michelin Star. The restaurant becomes famous, and not even two years later they receive a second Michelin Star.

Last year, the brothers opened a second restaurant in another part of the city.

A few months ago the big shock came. The brothers learned that their first restaurant had only received one Michelin Star; the second star was denied for unknown reasons.

A friend who works for a restaurant magazine revealed to the brothers that they got a star less, because they carried their soup in plastic bags from one restaurant to the other.

The brothers were very upset. All they could do is try to improve the business and also place new advertising. But somehow the information that the restaurant was carrying soup outside in bags had leaked to the public. One day they suddenly saw a sharp increase in their business. More orders than expected came in; the customers came in to buy soup to take away.

Every day it seemed, more requests for soup followed.

It looked like the best selling dish were the soups now. The brothers are convinced that negative news about the restaurant can be very good for business.

104. The Allotment

Unknown to many, German culture is also known for its allotments. Outside of the big cities, many people own small allotment plots which consist of a small garden and a small hut. Many of these allotments often form a small colony.

Most of the allotment owners are retirees and use it to escape from the inner cities.

One of these allotment owners is Wolfgang Meier, a pensioner from Hamburg. In his garden, he has built a small pond. He is very proud of his little goldfish that are swimming in the pond. Actually, Mr. Meier has no family and loves his fish. Every fish he has given a name.

One day, Mr. Meier visits his allotment and discovers a few of the fish dead on the surface. There's no explanation. Mr. Meier, however, is very sad and decides to sell his allotment. Strangely, nobody wants to buy his plot. Fortunately, a neighbor eventually buys his allotment for a very cheap price.

The neighbor is very happy with his plot and takes special care of it. After a short time, the allotment is in great condition. The garden is blossoming, and the pond is full of fish.

From time to time, Mr. Meier comes to visit his old allotment just to see what has changed. Mr. Meier is a bit jealous and he wishes to use his old allotment again.

One day, unexpectedly many dead fish are in the pond again.

A short time later, the new owner of the allotment receives a letter from Mr. Meier. It states that he, Mr. Meier would like to use the allotment on weekends. If he is allowed to use it for free, he would take care of the fish problem and guarantee that no more fish will die. On the other hand, he states that should his request be denied, he could imagine the problems becoming worse.

105. Inexpensive Shopping in Japan

My name is Rachel, and today I'm going to shop at the Japanese supermarket. As a student in Japan, I do not have much money and therefore must save on food. In addition, I support my mother in my home country. I mainly eat fish and vegetables. It's my so-called sushi diet. Luckily, these items are relatively inexpensive to buy in Japan. In the morning hours, the supermarkets are usually not as crowded. Today I need to buy rice, vegetables, tuna, and pasta. If I find something less expensive, I buy more. I buy only a little, which I feel means something more for the Japanese.

106. History - The First Humans

Most scholars still agree that the "African origin" model holds that all or nearly all modern human genetic diversity around the world can be traced back to the first anatomically modern humans to leave Africa.

The first Homo sapiens came out of North-East Africa, approximately 70 thousand years ago, and for at least 40,000 of those years, they obtained almost all of their food sources by hunting and gathering.

This species then migrated out of Africa along a coastal route via the Arabian Peninsula to South- and Southeast Asia, and eventually reached the Pacific and Australia. About 50 thousand years ago, the first modern humans, a subspecies of *Homo sapiens*, migrated from Africa to Asia Minor, and over the Caucasus to Europe; regarding the history of Modern humans reached Central Europe about 40 thousand years ago. Humans also migrated to the Americas about 15 thousand years ago; most came over the land-bridge which is now called the Bering Strait.

The 10th millennium BC saw the invention of agriculture and the beginning of the ancient era.

The Neolithic Age or New Stone Age was a period in the development of human technology, which included primitive tools beginning about 10,200 BC. Hunter-gatherers of that time had access to goods and tools that prehistoric hunter-gatherers did not have, due to trade with neighboring tribes and early agrarian societies. Most modern hunter-gatherers could already forge iron, making hunting and cutting tools of stones and bones which made primitive agriculture and hunting considerably easier.

www.ingramcontent.com/pod-product-compliance
Lightning Source LLC
Chambersburg PA
CBHW072155200426
43209CB00052B/1267